HOWZAT?

HOWZAT? takes a look at the club cricketer – how he plays and what happens to him.

Rain or shine he'll be out there on the pitch, practising tactics: strategies for handling fast bowling, for making friends with the umpire, for distracting the batsman. If these fail there is at least the opportunity to release pent-up emotions through the cricket ball. In the event passion and energy have been known to wipe the batsman from the field.

In this hilarious tour of the cricket pitch, Kevin Macey and Tony Benyon point out the vagaries of the whole team. HOWZAT? is not only a handy cricketing manual for anyone who sports whites in the season, but also an invaluable guide for the innocent bystander!

About the Authors

Kevin Macey was born in North London and educated at Highgate School and St Martin's School of Art. He has been a freelance cartoonist since 1974. He has worked for *Foul* magazine, the alternative football paper, *Time Out* and *The Times*. The publications to which he currently contributes include *The Health and Social Services Journal* and *The Times Literary Supplement*. He frequently does work for sports advertising. His advertising work also includes Fosters Lager, Nestles and Elastoplast.

Anthony Benyon attended the Hornsey College of Art where he studied industrial design. Before becoming a full time cartoonist he lectured at the Sir John Cass College of Art. He became a cartoonist for NME which has printed the cartoon strip *The Lone Groover* for many years. *The Lone Groover* has also seen life as a record, magazine, book, T shirt, radio sketches and badge. He has worked in most areas of the music business. Anthony Benyon is now a copywriter and art director in advertising.

Both authors live in London.

Kevin Macey & Tony Benyon

NEW ENGLISH LIBRARY
Hodder and Stoughton

Copyright © 1985 by Kevin Macey and
Tony Benyon
First published in Great Britain in 1985 by
New English Library
NEL Paperback Edition 1987

British Library C.I.P.

Macey, Kevin
Howzat?
1. Cricket – Anecdotes, facetiae, satire,
etc.
I. Title   II. Benyon, Tony
796.35'8'0207   GV919

ISBN 0-450-40942-2

Printed and bound in Great Britain for
Hodder and Stoughton Paperbacks, a
division of Hodder and Stoughton Ltd.,
Mill Road, Dunton Green, Sevenoaks,
Kent (Editorial Office: 47 Bedford
Square, London WC1B 3DP) by
St Edmundsbury Press Ltd.,
Bury St Edmunds, Suffolk.

CONTENTS

INTRODUCTION

An internationally renowned cricketer was invited to dinner
one Saturday night last summer by a friend of mine. He
arrived with his companion at 8 p.m. while outside it rained
cats and dogs, as it had been doing all day.
He was perplexed when his hostess informed him that my
friend had not yet returned from playing cricket.
The guest, on looking out at the weather, raised an eyebrow
and exchanged glances with his companion, suggesting his
host was up to no good.
Suddenly he smiled.
'Of course,' he said with relief. 'Club cricketers do that sort of
thing, don't they.'

Introduction

If you are not already a member of a cricket club and would like to join but feel your lack of experience at the game or lack of knowledge of the rules would hinder your entry, do not be concerned. Such apparent drawbacks have not hampered the playing members of many clubs and, in some cases, umpires.

The list below sets out the ten main reasons for joining a club. If you share any of the following passions or desires then you have all the potential required to make a successful player:

1. A desire for regular light exercise during the summer.
2. A love of fresh air.
3. A frequent desire to drink large amounts of alcohol.
4. A desire to escape from the family at weekends.
5. A need to provide an acceptable cover for clandestine meetings with the other woman (women).
6. A wish to belong.
7. An excuse to legally brutalise other human beings.
8. An excuse to be legally brutalised by other human beings.
9. To provide a platform for theatrical abilities not recognised by the drama club.
10. An undying passion for the world's greatest game.

CHAPTER 1

THE PLAYERS

MEETING
THE PLAYERS

The following pages describe the types of players you are likely to encounter either in your own team or opposing you. It is necessary to familiarise yourself with their idiosyncrasies. Befriending the wrong sort of chap on your first day could lead to severe problems.

Take heed! The players most eager to greet you are the ones nobody else will talk to. They are to be avoided. Remain detached from the onrush of the ostracised. Take your time and work out who the regular guys are. To start off drinking, by accident, with the team drunk could damage you physically. To attempt a conversation with the fast bowler could leave you with the impression that everyone else in the club is as unfriendly. Be careful!

You may be informed during your first week that you have not been selected for the team. Do not despair, attend the match fully kitted out. Immediately you arrive report to the Captain. Appear eager but not sycophantic when inquiring if any of the players have not turned up and if there is any chance of your having a game. Should the team be complete then curb your disappointment. Do not strike the bridge of the Captain's nose with your forehead, swear or throw a tantrum. Instead, merely shrug your shoulders while releasing a sigh and looking wistfully down-hearted.

Use this first match as an opportunity to observe the different

types who will soon become your comrades. Examine their
strengths and weaknesses. The latter, if exploited correctly,
will enable you to gain a regular team place.

THE DRINKER

Fortunately, cricket could have been and probably was invented as the ideal game to complement drinking. Not by accident does it attract some mighty imbibers. Teams have even been known to enrol a thirteenth man to transport and take care of the drinks kitty.

In most other sporting areas drinking or being sodden is a distinct disadvantage. In archery, the javelin and throwing the hammer it can be terminal. But for the seasoned sop it has been known to assist his batting.

Drink numbs the brain and deadens pain. Being struck by a fast bowler's bouncer is not something the drinker is aware of. His 16 or so pints before taking guard dismantles all his warning mechanisms of danger.

From the outset of many innings he sees the ball as large as a basketball and views the fast bowler at a reduced speed rather as a sober man views the six million dollar man in action or astronauts on the moon. On other occasions he may not see either ball or bowler, or at least three of both.

The Drinker is a compulsive slogger due to his ever-widening girth, his ability to see the ball and, more importantly, his need to have the game finished as early as possible to increase his drinking time and allow him a call of nature.

He is prone to being hearty and telling rambling vulgar stories again and again. Do not be concerned to leave him alone at the bar. He is unlikely to notice your absence.

The Drinker

THE HYPOCHONDRIAC

Every team is saddled with a hypochondriac. His appearance is misleading. Rather than being an anaemic weed he is tall, strongly built and apparently fit. One would think of him as an athlete if one did not know better.

It is his nature always to look for an illness or complaint as an excuse for playing poorly. If he has been bowling badly for several overs he automatically begins to limp and pauses to massage a suspected strain. Cricket being a summer sport it is no coincidence that he suffers from hay fever, or so he claims.

He does however make a fine close fielder. The smell of various ointments smeared over his body causes the batsman's eyes to stream. Laughter or nausea overtakes an opponent at the sight of him ramming an inhaler up each nostril in turn. More importantly, if he suspects himself to have acquired a new symptom when fielding he will ask the nearest player if he feels similarly. It is an off-putting question especially if the batsman is a fellow hypo.

When batting he is superb at breaking the bowler's concentration. During his run up the bowler will suddenly see the hypo collapse in the crease, clutching in the vicinity of a muscular spasm or due to a loss of balance caused by a suspected problem with his inner ear.

Never ask this man why he is late on match day. The reason could destroy your enjoyment of the day.

The Hypochondriac

THE YOB

The Yob is an integral part of the team. He is lewd, rowdy, coarse, vulgar, hot tempered, unreliable, obsessed by the opposite sex, prone to fisticuffs and damaging public houses. Curiously, he is not a leather-clad youth with a mohican haircut and tattooed scalp, but a middle-aged business man.

On his own and away from the club he is a different person, but in the team, on match day, he becomes a rabid beast. When returning from an away game he is always the one to moon at unsuspecting pedestrians.

During the match his behaviour is anarchic, disrespectful of rules, Umpires and decorum. His language is cluttered with oaths regardless of who is in attendance and he cannot move in the clubhouse without offending someone, starting an argument or pulling some crude practical joke.

Fortunately his reputation travels before him. Both Umpires and the opposing team will turn away and look falsely intent at passing swallows rather than confront him. The Yob's company is dangerous and boorish but on one of those occasions when you feel compelled to go out on the town and do some damage yourself he makes an excellent companion.

The Yob

17

THE BLEATER

The Bleater whines and complains at every opportunity and for any reason. The weather is either too hot or too cold, too wet or too dry and the opposition too strong, too weak, too serious or too light-hearted.

He is not the ideal man to be trapped with in a lift, but however much he drives you to despair it must be remembered that he is doing the same to the opposition. The Bleater is superbly disruptive. While batting he will draw the Umpire's attention to the bowler's 'suspect' action. Of course the bowler will not have a 'suspect' action, only a rising temper soon to be followed by a loss of line and length.

His bleating and snivelling complaints also grate on batsmen's nerves and often result in them assaulting the nearest fielder. Even Umpires driven to despair by his behaviour become disorientated and begin to make extraordinary decisions in his presence.

Whining about the price of beer, its opaque condition and lack of head, he sits alone in the bar. Grown men press themselves against the wall in the vain hope they will be invisible to him, barmen have nervous breakdowns and peanuts struggle to escape the confines of their bowl. He is a man fated to share his own company.

Why is he in the team? Simple, he is the only one willing to paint the sight screen and his father owns the best real ale freehouse within twenty miles of the ground.

The Bleater

THE POET

Certain players are drawn to cricket by a sense of romantic occasion, reared on John Arlott's wonderful descriptions. 'Willis, raw-boned, elbows pumping, knees audibly creaking . . .' – the poetry of the game described by a master. And so the dreamy-eyed aesthetic in brilliant whites skips up the pavilion steps with the sleeves of the pullover hanging casually behind him tied loosely around his neck, his head filled with thoughts of Sebastian.

Languidly he practises strokes in the summer light acting out a Noel Coward afternoon with shades of P. G. Wodehouse and desperately trying to catch a glimpse of his reflection in the clubhouse window.

The Poet is an Oxford spires type, best suited to punting up the river. He is a good sport who wants to 'play the game' and lie in long grass making daisy chains and reciting verse to a flush-cheeked Sloane Ranger who is washing her hair with apple-scented shampoo in a nearby stream.

He is not included in the team for his company nor for his unnerving presence in the showers. He is however good with words and has been allotted the task of supplying the local paper with match reports. These days a good press is so very important to the game.

The Poet

JIM (CAPTAIN)

Jim is the thinking Captain. Unfortunately he doesn't think hard enough and what he does think isn't really all that clever.

He does, however, have the correct thoughtful pose. Left hand supporting chin, brow furrowed and shirt collar turned up.

His attempts at keeping the batsmen on their toes by constantly changing the bowlers does not achieve success. In a limited over match he is often left with his best bowler having overs remaining. His declarations are also a disaster; no sane man declares during a limited over match played in fine weather.

The psychology of man management is not one of Jim's fortés either. His attempts at contrived sarcasm and forcefulness are usually met with him getting his box buckled by an irate bowler.

A pioneer of the helmet, Jim has often been the target of practical jokes (which he considers create a positive dressing-room atmosphere). Players have been known to place stickers on the front of his helmet without him knowing, stating for example 'All fast bowlers are Wallies'. Hospitalisation has followed but he always accepts his injuries philosophically.

Jim is Captain because he devotes his spare time to chasing up players and fixtures, and because the only alternative to him is that utter swine Adolf.

Jim (Captain)

ADOLF
(VICE CAPTAIN)

Adolf is so named because of the loud and sharp manner with which he issues his commands.

'That man! Two centimetres to the right! No! Not one! Not three! TWO!'

On those dreadful days Jim cannot captain the side Adolf stands rattling the ball bearings in his pocket and ferociously barking out his field placings. At other times, flicking his fingers and flexing his shoulders he tensely bowls imaginary balls and cuts the sort of figure usually sighted in the grounds of a lunatic asylum.

Only a team of highly trained psychiatrists could explain the reason why his face drains of colour and his sinews stiffen as he screams with venom ,'Wake up that man!'

when a ball drops thirty feet from a fielder.

Standing closer to the wicket than any other fielder, balls ricochet off his helmetless head to the boundary. His body is one vast bruise after batting, displaying the marks of balls he has refused to avoid. He exhibits his post match torso in the changing room with twisted pride, much to the disinterest of his team mates.

Adolf has become vice captain through fear and intimidation. Only the gallant Jim stands between him and the captaincy. At Christmas when the front wheel of Jim's car came off on the motorway everyone had their suspicions.

Adolf (Vice Captain)

THE HISTORIAN

The Historian is seeped in cricketing folk lore and legend.
He can quote with ease the batting averages or bowling
figures of any English International and supply a stream of
sleep inducing anecdotes to accompany them.
He is an expert on all local history connected with the game
but much to his disappointment he is a truly hopeless player.
Misguidedly he assumed by joining the club he would be
surrounded by like minds, but after many years he still fails to
realise this is not the case. Many players can recount with
stunning clarity the number of pints they imbibed ten years
ago at the 'Old Phelopians' match but cannot remember
the amount of runs they scored or the number of
wickets they took.
The Historian remains a most useful member of the team.
No one tackles the task of scoring with more vigour and more
competence. Glasses positioned towards the end of his nose
and hair straying academically hither and thither, he
becomes engrossed in reference books, slide rules and acres of
loose paper. Addressing nobody in particular he mutters
absent-mindedly that it is very fascinating. A. J. B. Dent is
the only batsman in the history of the club to have been out
for a duck in ten consecutive matches. His words, steered by a
late afternoon breeze, are carried to the boundary and
distributed to whichever blade of grass is interested.

THE LECHER

The Lecher uses cricket to veil his promiscuous sex life from his greatly mistreated wife. He is compulsively adulterous, a frequenter of lay-bys, car parks and the shrubbery nearest to the boundary.

Net practice and matches are the excuses he needs to be away from home without causing suspicion. The truth is he seldom turns up for either, but if his wife should telephone his attendance is confirmed although his presence is unobtainable. Why should other chaps devoid of his rampant amorality lie for him? The fact is the Lecher is a very fine player, capable of winning a match single-handed. He is a frustratingly natural player competent at any game demanding ball control, co-ordination and stamina.

A place in the team is always found for him whenever he turns up on match day. Like the drinker he plays with the same determination to end the match early, allowing him more time with the companion he has escorted to the ground. There are times his presence in the clubhouse creates tension. Wives and girlfriends are divided in their reactions towards him. Half wish to sneak to his wife about his behaviour while the others are curiously attracted by the indefinable charm he exudes. He is undoubtedly worth playing but equally worth watching.

The Lecher

THE JOVIAL CHAP

The Jovial Chap, like the fast bowler, is only useful in short bursts. An overdose of Mr. Jolly can lead to a depressing atmosphere in the clubhouse. No one wants to be continually glad they are alive. Otherwise the entire team would take to the field giggling and smiling like school girls. Easy meat for opponents like 'The Old Abbatoirians' or 'The Butchers and Livestock Management Eleven'.

The Jovial Chap has too much goodwill to claim a catch he hasn't taken, appeal for a doubtful LBW or stand eyeball to eyeball with an Umpire, threatening him with violence in the clubhouse if he gives him out.

He also commits the greatest of all sins by saying, 'It's only a game' to a player who at that moment would swop his home, car, career or children if only he could place his knee vigorously in an official groin.

When fielding, the Jovial Chap should be placed on the furthest boundary where his good nature can only lead to him giving the opposition the odd four he could have easily lied about.

His assets are his ability to strike the ball many a mile, his limitless ability to buy rounds, to lend money for fares home and to turn up full kitted and smiling during a nuclear attack.

He also excels in stopping fights which on many occasions one regrets having become involved in due to the unnatural and pugilistic ability of one's opponent.

The Jovial Chap

THE KNOW ALL

Captaincy in the hands of the 'Know All' would be a dangerous thing. Fortunately the first impression that this chap knows what he is talking about is soon exploded; he digs his own grave and expounds in it.

By one of those mysterious accidents of fate the 'Know All' is a reasonably good player. A sound bat, a dependable bowler and a useful fielder. It is unfortunate that like so many Radio Three commentators he is at his most knowledgeable and informative after the event.

'I wouldn't have done that . . .', 'I knew it, that decision was a mistake', 'What he should have done was . . .'

Such statements form the hard core of his conversation and mercilessly annoy his colleagues.

The 'Know All' is interested more in other players' techniques than his own, and his advice to them is as welcome as a Littlewood's cheque to a dying man.

'If I were you . . .' is an introductory phrase guaranteed to expel the recipient from the 'Know All's' vicinity, excused by an imaginary telephone call or last night's curry.

Curiously, he remains oblivious to the effect he has on other people but it is worth while keeping him as a team member.

He has been encouraged to give his advice on the wicket's condition and local knowledge to the visiting captain. When it is taken, the home team start the match with a distinct advantage.

The Know All

THE TALKER

The Talker is possessed with hyperactivity that manifests itself in the form of verbal diarrhoea. He is an unrestricted, compulsive gabber who cannot abide a pause in conversation in the clubhouse or at the crease.

A fast bowler attempts intimidation partly with soul burning glares of unbridled hostility, creating a still silence at the wicket in which the batsman is supposed to feel trapped and vulnerable. The Talker does not allow the silence to form, he tears it to shreds with staccato bursts of fragmented sentences as he attempts to snare his opponent in an irrelevant dialogue. He may even pursue the bowler back to his mark yapping at his heels.

He applies the same annoying technique when fielding close to the wicket. The blocker whose powers of concentration are legendary suddenly finds himself inundated with inquiries about his job, sex life and political leanings. This unsettling situation is unbearable for him and he resorts to the Umpire. The Umpire then becomes involved in a conversation with the Talker in which he is the junior partner.

Short, lean and jerky, the Talker endlessly seeks out a listening ear. If no receiver can be found his shadow or reflection may suffer his attention. He does, on rare occasions, say something interesting. But that only proves the law of statistics that a monkey, if placed long enough at a typewriter, will one day type out a line from a Shakespearean play.

34

The Talker

THE WIT

The Wit runs up to the wicket and bowls his most cunning ball, the tomato. It is so named because it is a tomato, a large red one that splatters against the bat and causes everyone on the field, apart from the batsman, to collapse with laughter. Unfortunately the Wit also places knickers in his teammates' bags, plastic flies in their beer and artificial dog dirt on the dressing room floor. His wit is not always appreciated.

A fast bowler will start his run up outside the boundary, steam up to the wicket like a wildebeest with an electric cattle prod embedded in its rear end and let go a screaming ball which rips off the wicket and howls past the Wit's ear, setting his sideburns alight. 'Okay!' says the batsman, 'Let's see your fast one!' The bowler's facial expression may not change, but behind his mask he dies a little.

The Wit is also an expert fielder. He executes the sigh and tut in the manner of a great Shakespearean actor, and when the batsman turns to identify his tormentor the Wit's upraised eyes, protruding tongue, red nose or electrically erect hair can have a devastating impact. Bowling however remains his forté. His grunts, sneers and expressions of exaggerated disgust when a batsman makes an error are unsurpassed. If you have not heard all his jokes, or witnessed his comedy routines before, he can be an entertaining teammate. Alas, repetition soon makes him grate on one's nerves, but the one small comfort is that someone, somewhere is suffering more than you, in this case his wife.

THE VISITING AMERICAN

Melvin the Visiting American steps lightly from the pavilion dressed in borrowed whites, a UCLA T-shirt and a green peaked cap. He grins, swings his bat high above his head and exudes boyish enthusiasm. The opposing bowler lifts an amused eyebrow and rubs the ball vigorously against his backside as the corners of his mouth salivate
with anticipation

Standing with bat held above his right shoulder, Melvin awaits his first ball. It flies off the wicket at waist height and with gusto Melvin improvises a baseball stroke that sends the ball bullet-like towards the boundary. Emitting a howl of unbridled glee he sets off for first base. Bowler and fielders alike raise their eyes to the heavens and groan. To be outplayed by a truly unorthodox player is a
wounding experience.

At first Melvin attempted to play the game correctly, but found himself too restricted. Now he scores as many runs as other average players, so why should he be concerned? After discovering 'cricket is all things to all people' he resorted to a natural style that has provided him with an inner sense of spiritual achievement. This philosophical approach came to him after reading *Zen and the Art of Motor Cycle Maintenance* and when he returns to the USA he plans to write a tome of his own entitled *Zen and the Art of Net Practice*.

THE WHEN-I

The 'When-I' is an atrociously arrogant snob. He plays the game as though he was the last English gentleman left alive and despises the more rowdy attitude of his teammates. The thought of playing with an American tortures his soul.

In the bar he drinks G and Ts while his colleagues are awash with ale, and loudly pontificates upon the decline of moral fibre. To him the national team is now filled with Hippies, Nancy Boys and other degenerates. In moments of increasing blood pressure he describes his mortification at witnessing another shabby rabble of colonials thrashing our spineless overpaid Internationals.

Walking stiffly to the wicket and humming 'Land of Hope and Glory' he clicks his boots together and takes guard. A conservative player by nature and breeding he plays safe shots and defends stoutly. On being dubiously dismissed he places the bat under his arm while removing his gloves and addresses the Umpire thus: 'Sir! You are no gentleman!'

Returning to the pavilion, curling his moustache and flattening stray hairs he remains unaware of the fielders who are lying on their backs, legs raised in the air and engulfed by hysteria.

He is named 'When-I' because of the way he begins each and every conversation 'When I was in India . . .,' 'When I was in the Civil Service . . .' etc.

41

ADVICE ON PLAYING

Later chapters offer specific advice on the specialist skills of bowling, batting and fielding. However, general hints can be given on appearing to be a competent player.

Appearance is in fact all-important. You must appear to be invisible, otherwise if you become noticed fellow players and your captain will become aware of your flawed game.

Looking the same as everyone else is essential. Do not, for example, wear brightly coloured socks with whites.

Watches are never worn during a match; they break, they distract the batsman's attention when worn by a bowler and if they are digital they have alarms that emit nauseating electronic bleeps on the hour. Jewellery is only worn by players who want to make a statement about their masculinity, or femininity. The fast bowler's gold medallion is as important to his image as the poet's pierced left ear.

Avoid sunglasses, dyed hair, ghetto blasters chained to your shoulder, lipstick and smoking. To fail to do so will mean you become noticed and your cover will be blown.

Faking the appearance of being a competent batsman is not too difficult. When emerging from the gloom of the pavilion do not look up at the sky to assess the weather conditions. If the sun is shining you will arrive at the wicket half-blinded. Do not look for mummy in the crowd and wave like a wet. Do not give the fielding side the V-sign or any other reason to feel hostile towards you. Never come out still fastening your pads,

without your bat, wearing an overcoat or reading a
newspaper. Emerge with your bat under your arm walking at
an even pace and looking down at the grass.

The Players

On arriving at the crease take guard and then walk halfway
down the wicket and prod it with your bat. Raise your bat to
waist height and look around at the field placings, then tug at
your cap, adjust your box and prepare for the first ball.
By this stage only you will know of your inability to score a
single run. All will be discovered if you have not practised to
perfection at least one text book stroke. Whatever ball is
bowled you must play this stroke. A miracle may occur and it
may be the correct stroke for the ball, but this is most
unlikely. After you have been bowled, caught or out LBW
put the blame immediately onto the state of the wicket,
movement behind the bowler or being unsighted. Deflect
attention away from your incompetence. To have groped
after the ball unstylishly would certainly have left you
discovered. This way you may get another game.
The unfortunate aspect of fielding is that wherever you try to
hide the ball seeks you out and the more hopeless you are the
more often the ball flies in your direction.
Stopping the ball and returning it are the main skills to learn.
Catching it is a bonus. The ball is hard, very hard, and when
it hits you the pain is extremely acute. You must keep the fact
that you are playing a game of cricket foremost in your mind
on even the most soporific afternoon. To be daydreaming and
suddenly wake to see the ball flying in your direction does not
allow you time to work out logically where you are and what
you are doing. Instinctively you may, at the beginning of the
season, assume you are playing football and leap and head
the ball. I have seen this mistake occur; it was not an

attractive sight.

Balls travelling at high speed along the ground are more deadly than those airborne. You can feign an attempted dive at a ball in mid-air and miss it to everyone's satisfaction but the grass cutter has to be stopped. To miss it would make you appear whimpish. Never try to stop it with your hands; bones are brittle and they snap easily. Always use the blocking boot while shouting 'Violinist' or 'Surgeon'. Everyone will understand.

Bowling is something you will not have to do, unlike batting and fielding, unless you play twenty overs a side and each player has to bowl two overs. If this is the case you must play to your strengths even if you do not possess any. To bowl at speed or spin is foolish if you have neither.

Bowl little ones as accurately as possible off a short run. Do not attempt to intimidate the batsman with ribald remarks or threatening gestures; get the over completed as quickly as possible. You may feel the underarm ball is your natural style, but avoid bowling in this manner at all costs.

Begin to limp and massage an imaginary calf strain some minutes before you are due to bowl or grope on the field for a lost contact lens but remain artificially eager to bowl. If you should be hit for consecutive sixes off your first two balls do not break down and weep, continue the over and then walk away shaking your head. Appear to disbelieve what has just occurred and exaggerate the fact by bowling imaginary balls in the field still shaking your head with bewilderment.

48

CHAPTER 2

THE BATSMEN

THE AGGRESSIVE BATSMAN

Cricket, to the aggresive batsman, is not a game. It is a therapy aimed at ridding him of repressions originating from either his childhood or his diminutive stature.

Shredding the cherry, crippling a close fielder, driving the ball back into the bowler's groin, flesh wounding an umpire or stunning a passing pigeon all help to fulfil his vendetta against nature.

Bowling a bouncer at this man is an affront to his very being; not for him ducking and weaving. Balls may ricochet off his body at countless miles an hour but he will show no sign of pain, not even rub the stinging bruise. Instead his eyes narrow and his hirsute forearms bristle as he chews even more ferociously on the half pound wad of gum crammed behind his curling lip.

The only other team member with his command of spine numbing oaths and personal abuse is the fast bowler. Indeed, these two players are kindred spirits. Their dark brows and hairy chests may often be seen knitted together in the bar, medallions glinting and shirts matchingly unbuttoned as they brood over a shared sense of victimisation.

A hard drinker, a crasher of fast cars, this man is only a good mixer in the context of a brawl.

The Aggressive Batsman

THE SLOGGER

The Slogger rolls to the crease with flush red cheeks and mighty forearms. Dressed in a marquee sized shirt and armed with a jumbo sized bat he stands his ground, a mountain of a man against whom Falstaff would seem no more than a toothpick.

The Slogger slogs the ball many a mile, being so grossly overweight no other option is available to him. To attempt running for a single would be foolish and a three could be terminal. His great bulk determines he must reach the boundary with every stroke. Standing as though rivetted to the crease he swings his mighty weapon and greets the encroaching ball with explosive results or, as is often the case, he is dismissed first ball. If he should remain the scoreboard becomes a fast moving blur and even the most doubtful victory is dreamt of as a possibility.

In full cry he thrills all those spectators who have not parked their cars too close to the boundary to be dented and smashed. He is less appreciated by those living adjacent to the ground who have greenhouses.

A heavy man, he is popular in the bar where he consumes vast amounts of ale. A good listener, a great laugher, he is, alas, a hopeless, immobile fielder unless placed at forward short leg where the ball has problems avoiding his bulk and may embed itself in a fold of his quivering flesh.

The Slogger

THE BLOCKER

Drawn, tense and tight-lipped the Blocker opens the innings
with a customary dead bat, held by relaxed hands at 45
degrees to the wicket. The angle of his bat becomes more
acute as the match progresses until he merely traps the ball.
He is a defensive or boring player depending on which part of
the country you come from.

Helmeted with arm pads, front and back torso pads, a
reinforced box and a gum shield, he resembles the tiny
aniseed ball at the centre of a gobstopper. What remains
visible of his face demonstrates a range of facial expressions
similar to those of a brick wall.

Between balls he clenches his fists and scratches desperately
at the crease like an agitated hen. Beneath the padding he is
not a happy man; some dark secret seems hidden within him
casting gloom over the game. He is not a man for whom joy
and friendship have any meaning. His sunken eyes behind
bi-focals see only his own reflection and the ball forever
coming at him.

While men and wickets fall around him the Blocker plays on.
The opposition try to give him singles to get him down to the
other end, but the only singles he takes are at the end of each
over, to keep the strike. The innings finished he carries his bat
and a score of twenty runs back to the pavilion where he
dresses and then unspeaking leaves for home, alone, much to
everyone else's relief.

The Blocker

THE TWITCHER

Lean from burning nervous energy the Twitcher is a perfect match for any bowler. After delivering a thunder bolt the fast bowler stalks moodily back to his mark and arriving at the boundary he is unsettled to see the Twitcher, who has also gone walkabout doing pressups on the pavilion steps after three laps of the car park and a quick shower.

The fast bowler may well deliver the ball at nearly ninety miles an hour but it still provides the Twitcher enough time to go onto the back foot, onto the front foot, onto the back foot again, smile, wipe his nose, shuffle across the crease and still

56

The Twitcher

edge the ball through the slips for a boundary.
Tempers fray while he is at the wicket. His afflictions are
contagious. He touches his pads, adjusts his box, tugs his
cap, pushes stray hairs beneath it and reassures himself that
his medallion is in place, over and over again. Finally the
fielders and Umpires find themselves uncontrollably copying
him, and from a distance the game appears to have been
invaded by mosquitoes.

His enthusiasm and application make him popular in the
clubhouse although his team mates acknowledge they do not
know him well. He is never in the same place long enough for
anyone to get to know him.

THE STROKE MAKER

The Stroke Maker is set apart from other men. He descends the pavilion steps with the air of a county trialist. He looks like every good player should, handsome profile, an athletic body and a suggestion of feline grace in his casual stride. Walking to the wicket with an air of detached arrogance he plays a dazzling array of practice strokes, causing gasps of admiration from the spectators. A buzz of excitement also stirs among the fielders as they note he possesses the fashionable bat of the moment, currently a V12.

To the first ball he receives he plays an elegantly effortless straight bat. The remaining balls of the over are greeted by the same precise stroke, but between overs he demonstrates a cluster of perfect cover drives.

Next over he actually executes the cover drive. The ball flies off the edge of his V12 catching second slip by surprise and almost removing his head before travelling at speed to the boundary. The Stroke Maker shakes his blonde hair in amused disbelief and once more takes immaculate guard.

Next ball he plays an even more perfect cover drive. Unfortunately the stroke occurs several centimetres from the ball which removes the off wicket.

Rehearsing the stroke and to shouts of 'Hard Luck!' he casually saunters back to the pavilion. One would assume his

The Stroke Maker

early dismissal to be a rare and astonishing occurrence. In fact, in five seasons he has scored only one fifty but no other player is ever dismissed more elegantly.

ADVICE ON BATTING

Running Between the Wickets

Calling for a run only when the ball is in front of you makes sense when printed in a text book. In practice this is not the case. If the ball is behind you and the call becomes the responsibility of your fellow batsman, take no notice of him. In the case of Club Cricket he may well be drunk, stoned, watching a sunbathing nymphet on the boundary, unfamiliar with the rules, myopic or in favour of your dismissal because of an argument you had the previous evening. Don't under any circumstances trust him.
Never be pressured into running. On occasions you may be batting with a Twitcher who arrives at your end of the wicket and shouts 'Yes!' while the ball is still in flight. If this happens shout 'No!' and play the shot.
If the Twitcher should race back to the other wicket, observe the stroke you've played, shout 'Yes!' and begin to run, wait

Advice On Batting

The Batsmen

Advice On Batting

for him to arrive, then grab him by his lapels, pull him
towards you, stare deeply into his eyes and say quietly 'No!'.
By this time he will be out and no longer a problem to you.
Always call 'Yes!' or 'No!'. To call 'What do you think John?'
leads to a conversation and impairs running.
When a fellow batsman is blessed with a stutter run him out
at the first opportunity even if it means tripping him up half
way down the wicket.
If the ball is in the hands of either the wicket keeper or the
bowler it is inadvisable to run, to still be running or to be at
the same end of the wicket as your partner.
Should you be standing by your fellow batsman at one wicket
while the bails at the other end of the wicket are being
removed, this means one of you is out. A decision must be
made, preferably in your favour. Be the first one to speak,
'John, you utter wally, you could have made a fifty today,
hard luck mate!' is the best psychological move. He will be
half way back to the pavilion before he realises you
ran him out.

On Being Given Out

When a dubious decision or a good decision is given against you, refuse to acknowledge it. If your stumps lie spread out on the ground, state loudly and confidently that you understood the Umpire to have shouted 'No ball!' and anyway you were not ready, besides several small boys had been pushing the sightscreen away during the bowler's run up.

Confident, instant reactions are the best deceit. If the ball contacts the edge of your bat, flies to first slip and is caught, immediately drop to the ground clutching your arm and scream out that it's broken.

When struck soundly on the pads, before an LBW decision can be given drop to the ground clutching your box and shout loudly words to the effect that you are dying.

After hitting a ball to cover that is obviously going to be caught, immediately collapse onto the stumps claiming to have been shot by an air gun pellet. There is a good chance cover may be distracted and miss the catch. If not the Umpire will be uncertain of the law concerning batsmen and air guns.

Advice On Batting

Reacting to Intimidation

If it is sunny and close fielders are brought in, complain to the Umpire about shadows being cast onto the wicket. If it is raining, complain that fielders are dripping onto the wicket. If it is cloudy, complain the fielders are talking to you. Should these complaints not work try hitting the ball hard at a fielder's shins or over-emphasise your stroke in an attempt at bringing your bat into contact with his body. This is known as spreading the field.

Advice On Batting

Faced by an intimidating fast bowler hurling bouncers at you it is best to fall screaming to the ground whenever the ball makes contact with you. It is a reaction designed to gain the Umpire's sympathy.

Lying down and moaning 'God! I knew I was playing too soon after my operation', 'Oh no! I think my stitches have opened!' or 'Three months to live and this happens!' may work in your favour. Pretending not to be hurt when you are is an unnecessary waste of pain.

The Batsmen

The last resort when being intimidated by a fast bowler is to threaten him with reciprocal violence. This action is desperate and only works if you are over six feet six inches high and have a karate black belt. To wear a black belt holding up your flannels is a suitable aggressive signal. Combined with a lingering Clint Eastwood glare it could result in throwing some doubt into the bowler's mind. Sony Walkmans are excellent for boosting confidence. Taking guard to 'Chariots of Fire' can provide a boost of adrenalin and a sensation of immortality. The fielders cannot complain about you wearing headphones any more than they can about a deaf batsman. It does not interfere with the game and fills in moments of tedium while batting with a Blocker. Headphones of course impair calling but that, as we already know, is an imperfect practice. Praying at the crease before taking guard can upset some bowlers as they ponder the consequences of wounding a religious man. Bringing small children with you to the wicket and kissing them fondly goodbye as though for the last time can also make a fast bowler lose his appetite for the sight of blood.

THE TOKEN ALL ROUNDER

In most teams there is one player who is good at all games without ever trying. He instinctively plays above par snooker, darts, golf or football and bowls, bats and fields with the confidence of a natural athlete to whom nothing appears difficult. He can outdrink the drinker, eat the hottest Saturday night curry with no Sunday after effects, drive a fast car competently and effortlessly seduce the most sought after girl in the room.

These qualities make him superficially the most popular player in the club house. But deep down other players despise him more than anyone else on the planet. Should he fail with bat and ball certain dark hearts are lifted to levels of exquisite ecstasy.

The all rounder's most annoying characteristic is his failure to realise how good he is or the frustration he creates in others. 'A waste of natural talent' is the most common description applied to him when he is seen at the bar or enjoying life away from the wicket.

His joviality and unconcern are regarded as being immaturity and provide him with more nicknames than other players. 'Nessy' or 'Batman' are labels that imply a mocking tone. Fortunately he is too thick to realise what is going on. He accepts his abilities in the same way others accept their limitations. Never lend him any money, you will never see it again.

The Token All Rounder

CHAPTER 3

THE BOWLERS

THE TWEAKER

The Tweaker is a left arm spinner. If he was any good he would be playing for England. The fact is that he plays extremely erratically and so plays club cricket. Erratic bowling, however, is the most dangerous of all to a batsman. If the bowler doesn't know where the ball is going when it leaves his hand what chance does a batsman have?
Setting a field on the offside and then firing five balls down the legside makes the batsman uneasy. He can only assume the bowler is a master tactician luring him into a trap or a complete wally bowling for the first time. When the sixth ball shoots out from the back of the bowler's hand, flies skywards and on the offside the batsman's suspicions are compounded.
The captain never displays a lack of faith in the Tweaker. When he bowls yet another dire ball he nods his head approvingly and claps enthusiastically. Falling onto the ground and thrusting a boot into his mouth would be a giveaway and make the batsman realise he is confronted by a complete clown.
The Tweaker is a portly little chap who tries very hard to appear a thinking person. He will come out with profound statements such as 'Morning mist turns the afternoon' and pretends he can read wickets and the weather better than anyone else. Do not trust him even when he is reading a train timetable.

The Tweaker

THE FAST BOWLER

The Fast Bowler is the team's cruise missile, the ultimate answer to opening batsmen. Somewhere in the countryside he starts his run up. Pounding the earth he appears on the boundary. Gasping for air he arrives at the wicket releasing a meteoric delivery. In mid-air he twists his malevolent form into a grotesque swirl of splayed limbs and his bull neck thrusts out as he roars a flame-edged appeal 'HOWZAT?'

Most times the Umpire, suffering buckled knees and ruptured ear drums, raises a trembling finger. If not, the fast bowler muttering purple oaths, tugs his sweat soaked shirt away from his body, adjusts his medallion and returns from whence he came. Unfriendly, bitter, with red stained thighs and dripping wrist bands he continues his revenge on life. The Club Cricketer Fast Bowler is an explosion of hostility in his first stint, but when called back for his second he has stiffened. The hutch by then open is saved from his most terrifying venom. Such is his eternal torment and such is the reason for his simmering, lonely image.

Image is all important to the Fast Bowler. In the steak house he eats raw meat with his hands. In the bar he drinks beer from the bottle, after biting off the top and eating his glass.

THE PLOPPER

The Plopper is so called because of his ability to 'plop' the ball on a perfect length and line six balls out of every over. Each delivery is of slow to even slower pace with little variation off the wicket.

Drifting into the sunset of his playing days with grey hair, rotund shape and anachronistic creamy kit, he appears a figure of ridicule to opposing players.

The Plopper marks out his run, turns on his heels and mumbles to himself as he flutters gnarled fingers in the direction of fielders as though counting them. Several tortuous strides later he releases the ball, which is duly driven to the boundary 'a little uppish but quite safe'. Next ball the batsman is out caught at cover after playing across the line. Sooner or later, everyone is out playing across the Plopper's line. For this reason he is the team's leading wicket taker, averaging a hundred wickets a season.

In cricket as in life all is not what it seems and the Plopper proves the rule 'give a man enough rope and he'll tie himself in knots'.

In the pavilion the Plopper is an equally moderate drinker of half pints, a quiet nodder, a philosopher whose knack of taking wickets makes the 'fast bowler' chew the studs of his boots with frustrated envy.

The Plopper

THE TRUNDLER

It is almost impossible to write anything about the Trundler.
If Clark Kent tears off his suit he reveals a leotard with
'Superman' written on it, but if the Trundler tore off his suit
he would be wearing a leotard with 'Anonymous Man'
written in grey paint on a greyer background.
To describe him as being the Workhorse of the team would
not be unkind. He is happiest running up a hill in a strong
wind and driving sleet. The only way for a batsman to be out
to him is by being a complete idiot or by falling asleep.
Polishing the ball philosophically he tucks his loose shirt into
baggy flannels that look likely to fall to his ankles at any
moment. With measured stride he completes his run up and
bowls a ball of average speed and line which does nothing
either through the air or off the wicket. Devoid of the
Plopper's accuracy the ball is promptly drilled for four by a
grateful batsman.
The Trundler is in his forties, average height, pinkish, a
balding head with flattened strands of hair brushed across it,
the suggestion of a beer gut and the face of a loyal basset
hound. Even though he makes an appallingly bad number
eleven he is liked by everyone and regarded as a reliable,
trustworthy Yeoman. What dark secret is this man hiding? Is
he cooking the firm's books or is he a KGB agent?

The Trundler

ADVICE ON BOWLING

Appealing

Each bowler has his own highly personalised style of appealing. The Tweaker, who projects an image of experience and cunning, is a subtle appealer. When his first dubious case of LBW occurs he turns to face the Umpire and inquires almost in a whisper. Being the first appeal the Umpire automatically turns it down. Unbelievably the Tweaker returns to his mark, nodding his head and muttering 'Good decision'.

The Tweaker repeats this process several times, lulling the Umpire into a false sense of security until the next appeal when he falls onto one knee as he turns to face the official. 'On my mother's life, how was that? I mean was that or was that not plum?' he screams. The Umpire who in all probability has been daydreaming is so shaken that his finger rises in a reflex action.

The Fast Bowler, as we already know, climbs highest, remains airborne the longest and appeals loudest. The unarmed Umpire's only form of defence is his finger and he raises it in ratio to the blood-curdling appeals he receives.

The Fast Bowler is also an excellent post-appeal

HOW

expressionist, pounding the wicket with his fists or gnawing at the stumps when he is turned down. He is also the most informative in displaying with a flourish the direction the batsman should take to the pavilion.

The Trundler through his honesty and innocence is also a successful appealer. When his slips rise to hysterically inquire for a dubious LBW the Trundler, always determined to see fair play, will turn them down himself. 'No way Umpire, I can't ask for that'. The Umpire immediately feels a warm glow as he realises someone is at last on his side. A relationship based on trust is formed. Wanting to cement the new friendship the Umpire will force the Trundler to accept the next appeal, not willing to upset the Umpire he reluctantly agrees, and so the afternoon goes.

The Plopper, because of his great age, has usually known the Umpire for a long time. He does not bother with dramatic appealing, shouting, weeping or begging. The following conversation takes place:

Umpire: What do you think?
Plopper: Damn close, John.
U . . . I reckon it would have had off stump.
P . . . It was low enough, too.
U . . . Well?
P . . . How was that?
U . . . OUT!

If the Umpire should be new the Plopper is of great help in

WAS

giving him advice, and before the game is over he is totally reliant on him.

If fate has conspired to make you an undemonstrative chap unable to appeal with any kind of conviction you need special help. Drama classes will be able to assist you in voice projection, clarity of diction, volume control and accompanying body movements.

The very words, 'Howzat?' can imply much, for example, 'You are awake Umpire, aren't you?' or 'Only a complete fool could possibly turn down such a dead cert!' or 'What on earth are you doing under that white coat you degenerate, be smart, give the decision in my favour and I won't draw it to the others' attention'. Note the emphasis on the Umpire's weaknesses and natural sense of persecution.

Body movements and facial expressions only become important when the decision is against you. One look through half-closed eyes should be enough to make the Umpire realise he has made a grievous mistake. Similarly the batsman must be made to realise he has escaped by the skin of his teeth, that his luck will not last and next ball he will be exposed as the incompetent idiot he so obviously is.

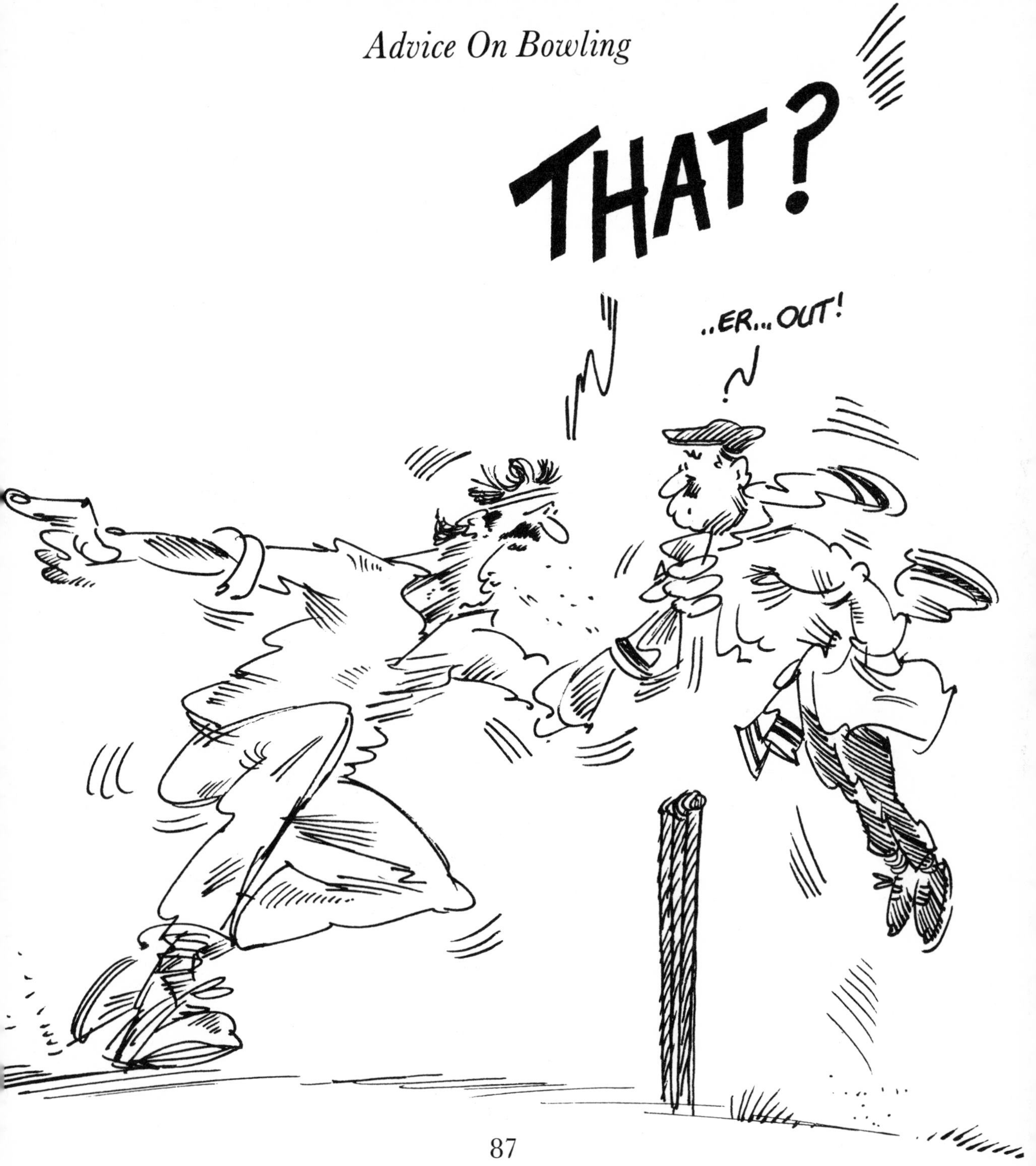
THAT?
..ER...OUT!

CHAPTER 4

THE
FIELDERS

THE KEEPER

Occasions frequently occur when a harmless dolly catch will be dropping into the Keeper's welcoming gloves. At this moment a vision appears in his mind of the catch having been completed and him holding the ball high above his head and triumphantly appealing. Preoccupied with this vision he attempts to catch the ball and simultaneously inquire, resulting in an unsightly fumble and a dropped catch.

On other occasions he anticipates the line of the ball and diving to the offside he manages to stop the ball on the leg side with a trailing boot.

Wanting to look magnificent in full flight is his major downfall. At the end of the season he would rather have one good photograph of himself diving outstretched and parallel to the ground than a harvest of unspectacular nicks reaped down the offside.

The pursuit of the spectacular catch has led to him being the most superstitious player on the team. Between balls he touches the bails, his St. Christopher, his pads and the lucky crow's foot in his back pocket. In between overs he must run to the other wicket, touch his toes six times, lean to the right, then to the left ten times and perform a dozen knee bends and press-ups. These superstitions often lead to him being mistaken for an eager health fanatic. This is not the case, he is simply a neurotic in good physical condition.

The Keeper

THE SLIPS

The Slips are cricket's choreographed chorus line. Their routine is practised to perfection and performed in unison. From a standing position they lean forward and place their hands on their knees. Bending their legs they stretch their hands with palms opened upwards in front of them. Shouting they leap into the air with arms outstretched. On landing they shake their heads vigorously, raise their eyes upwards, spit and resume a standing position. The routine is performed six times every over, not allowing the extra balls.

Equally important to the body movements are the loud noises they emit. On being air borne they yell 'HOWZAT!' on landing they either yell 'What?' or 'Nice one!' depending on the position of the Umpire's finger. Of course the dialogue does change when the routine is performed on different stages throughout the world.

HOWZAT?

THE OUTFIELD

On Catching the Ball

Catches tend to descend on the boundary fielder from a great
height. To take one's eyes off the ball when it is falling at
speed can be fatal. At this moment ignore all girlish shouts
from beyond the boundary such as 'Can you help fix my bra
strap', 'Want to rub sun tan lotion on my body?' or just
'Yoohoo big boy!' They are all ploys devised to make you lose
your head.
Never be tempted to fall in love with a boundary nymphet.
They are sirens positioned to lure you out of position.
On no account stand on the boundary with a cigarette in one
hand and a pint of beer in the other. When called upon for
swift action you will not know which to put down first. The
decision can often be made too late.
Looking up at the ball and waiting to catch it with your hands
raised above your face is a mistake. If you have butter fingers
you could end up with minced chops.

The Outfield

On Stopping the Ball

Occasionally you will have to make a diving stop. Before hurling yourself full length to save a grass cutter make sure all half bricks, broken bottles and dog dirt have been removed from the area you patrol. A rolling stone may gather no moss but a rolling cricket ball picks up dog dirt with ease. But nothing is worse than diving head first into a mound of canine nasty.

A stout pair of reinforced boots are more useful than ungloved hands for stopping a well struck ball. Avoid using your head or other vulnerable parts of your body. If you are nervous don't be afraid of wearing your box on the boundary but pads, crash helmets and baseball gloves are frowned upon.

The Outfield

THE INFIELD

On Fooling the Batsman

When the first few balls are driven in your direction always react slowly and after returning the ball clutch your thigh or back suggesting you have a painful muscular condition. The batsman will be lulled into a false sense of security and will soon attempt two runs where only one is safe. Pounce swiftly onto the ball and send it rocketing to the Keeper for a run out.

This may be gamesmanship but after all it is only a game. A fast ball shooting along the ground is as unpredictable as a mad heifer. It could strike a molehill or stone and fly either upwards to the right or to the left just as you reach to pick it up. If this should happen and the ball passes you, pretend to have picked it up and to throw it in. The batsman will automatically falter and you may save a run. He will of course dislike you bitterly from then on and want to get the better of you at the earliest opportunity. Next time a similar grass cutter explodes towards you make the pick up if possible but pretend it's passed by. Turn as though to follow the ball, continue turning and return the ball at speed. The batsman will be eager to show you up and will have begun to run. If you are accurate with your throw he will be out. Another variation of the method above is to pretend the ball has passed by when it is concealed under your fallen body. Sit

up holding a hand above your eyes and looking towards the boundary. Curse loudly, wait for the batsman to run and throw the ball.

CHAPTER 5

THE UMPIRES

ASSESSING THE UMPIRE'S ABILITY

The visiting team is supposed to bring its own Umpire. If he is unknown to you it is essential to assess his abilities and character as early as possible. This can be done by whispering 'Got any nude photographs of your wife?' as you pass close to him. The usual response to this inquiry is a startled 'No!' to which you reply 'Want to buy some?'

If the Umpire falls into this trap and then reacts to being caught out by blushing and looking down at his feet it is a sign that he is an utter wimp and will be easy to bully. Should he laugh loudly and slap you on the back it means he is a jolly good sport.

If he refuses to acknowledge that a joke has been made, wags a reproving finger and lectures you, then beware, he goes by the book and cannot be taken advantage of. Should he respond with a similar lack of humour by hitting you, then avoid him for the rest of the afternoon.

If the Umpire fails to understand the joke at all, looks furtively around the field and asks where you got the photographs then he is deeply unsure of himself and his wife; he will be easy to confuse. Should he reply 'Yes thank you!' to the first part of the joke and smirk confidently at you, then realise you have been caught out by an alert and agile mind. Do not take liberties with this man. In all probability he has the weaponry to humiliate you.

Assessing the Umpire's Ability

THE INEPT UMPIRE

An official Umpire may fail to turn up on match day. If this happens a substitute has to be found who is acceptable to both home and visiting players. Necessity is often the mother of selection and a regular player may be forced to switch roles if a likely candidate cannot be plucked from the spectators or clubhouse. These are the biased, inept or bizarre Umpires, the ones who in their enthusiasm have been known to take catches, field the ball themselves, give out a batsman although no appeal has been made and shout 'Yes!' to encourage a timid batsman to run.

If he shows an overt bias towards your team under no circumstances feel guilty. His preference must be exploited to your best advantage. Work at his weaknesses. If he is a drinker carry a hip flask. If he is a talker, talk to him and take every opportunity to help him make a decision. The opposition may feel victimised, but deep down they will know that the circumstances could easily be reversed.

Should the visitors cunningly contrive the selection of their own man never allow the situation to make you hostile towards him. Stroke his ego, tell him how well he is performing. Puffed up with self importance he may be dissuaded from his bias and even enjoy the fact he is being considered 'fair-minded'. When a man takes the centre of the stage and is endowed with power he can become the most dreadful ham actor, and peculiar changes of character take place; witness the House of Commons.

104

The Inept Umpire

THE AGGRESSIVE UMPIRE

Hitlers will never under any circumstances give a man or beast the benefit of the doubt. They exist solely not to be taken advantage of and all of them suffer acute persecution complexes. It is foolish to argue with these men as any disagreement on your part is regarded as a personal attack on them.

The only chance you have to influence their decisions is to work a scam on them when you are fielding. The most successful of these is the 'Williams Technique'. Named after S. D. P. Williams who first used the ploy, S. D. P. Williams used his brother R. C. Williams as a scape-goat. Noting they had a particularly harsh Umpire on match day S.D.P. rehearsed his brother R.C. in the role of grumbling agitator. When R.C. whined his first complaint on the field S.D.P. sprang into action with a barked reprimand. 'Williams! Don't question the Umpire' followed by, 'Williams! Show the Umpire some courtesy!' Quite naturally the Umpire felt flattered by the respect being shown to him. When R.C. appealed unpleasantly for LBW after the ball struck a batsman's hip and was taken behind S.D.P. turned on him with venomous chastisement, 'Williams, don't ever appeal for an obviously ridiculous LBW again! Can't you see it's a clear catch behind?' Turning to the Umpire he inquired 'Howzat?' The Umpire did not falter. Feeling his level of elevated importance might be impaired by alienating

S.D.P., he immediately raised his finger.
Batting is a different matter. You really have no chance with
a Hitler apart from prayer or luck.

108

CHAPTER 6

THE CLUB

ACTIVITIES

The most important function of the Clubhouse, if your team is lucky enough to possess one, is to provide the match day tea. This is conjured up by wives and sweethearts and can fluctuate from the disgusting to the over-satisfying. Cakes and sandwiches form the hard core of an average tea. On a hot afternoon the excessive consumption of these delicacies can lead to sleepiness in the field or, more dangerously, when batting.

Annual social functions also take place in the Clubhouse, such as the exotic Christmas Disco or Dinner. It is best to remain sober on these occasions because of the attendance of such dignitaries as the Club President and his boozing mates who have come to rub shoulders with the star players while ignoring the rest. By remaining sober you can resist being drawn into embarrassing behaviour such as seducing the President's wife or throwing bread rolls at an appalling guest speaker.

By keeping a clear head you can negotiate these minefields and avoid tarnishing your reputation. Besides, there are many Brownie points to be scored by finding the President's trousers, being the only one able to drive the dignitaries home and by ensuring those players who have got on your wick all year get themselves truly in it, preferably up to their necks.

Activities

THE BAR

The Bar is the post match refuge if the bar bores can be avoided. They are the members who no longer play or have never played. They are all too eager to provide you with the benefit of their knowledge which in nearly all cases is acutely unbeneficial.

The bores are easily spotted. They are the only chaps in the bar demonstrating strokes or who start conversations with the phrases 'When I was playing . . .' or 'If I can just say one thing . .' and 'If it wasn't for my injury . . .'. What follows can fray a strong man's temper.

If you do feel in a mood to sink a few beers more than usual, only do so if your fellow players are swilling them around you. To be the only one in a state of paralysis can be dangerous. You may find yourself cold, waking up in the bar at 2 am in the dark and semi-dressed.

Most bars have a rota for players to serve behind the counter. You should be as unenthusiastic as everyone else to take your turn. The team drunk is the best man for the job. At least you will get large measures.

Take the earliest opportunity to learn the favourite club songs and join in with the singing. You may find that by doing so you appear to have become one of the 'oiks' you have always despised. Smugness may lead you to believe you are only playing a role. Do not be deceived, they all think this.

The Bar

THE DRESSING-ROOM

Away dressing-rooms are bare, inhospitable places. They are designed to be so. Why should any right-minded person offer the opposition comfort?

After putting on your whites you will be left wondering what to do with your valuables. The Umpire is the most likely candidate to guard your watch and money if you don't own a motor car with reinforced glove compartment. Make sure the Umpire signs a receipt. Not that he may be untrustworthy, but it stops less honest players claiming they have left priceless fob watches with him and demanding compensation.

Once the game is over a shower will be needed. If you are playing away be prepared for a cold shower. Dressing-rooms are designed to provide the home team with all the hot water.

Never appear shy or behave oddly on your first time in the showers. It is important for other players not to develop any suspicions about you. Similarly, when stripping off your clothes do so nonchalantly and don't be seen wearing over-decorative underwear. If you have tattooes wear elastoplasts over them until you know everyone better.

As a new boy it is advisable not to have a brand new kit and a pair of unused boots. Being the recipient of sniggering will put you off your game. It is your first game, survive it.

The Dressing-Room

THE PITCH

Pitches may be the flat green velvet of which dreams are dreamed or semi-sloping scrubland. They may or may not have sightscreens. If they do have screens of the wooden type never volunteer to paint them. It is a job no one performs other than the hyperactive enthusiast or the youngest and most easily bullied member of the team.

Before the match commences take time to survey the pitch, removing any sharp objects you may find and noting the location of any steaming mounds left by neighbouring dogs. Standing by the wicket apparently trying to read how it will play is an act of extreme naffness. Only International or County players pose in this manner. All you may find to read is a Sunday newspaper or a sweet wrapper being blown across the ground.

Note if the pitch is near a main road or a river. Should it be bounded by either obstacle ensure you do not have to perform in the outfield. No sensible person wants to retrieve boundaries from fast flowing water or traffic all afternoon. Similarly, if you are to bowl you will want to know the wind's direction, where the sun will be and what windows or wet roofs may reflect into a batsman's eyes.

When batting always hit the ball in the direction of mole hills, nettles, thistles, cow pats or any other obstacles that may hinder retrieving the ball. It is of utmost importance to make the best use of the Pitch.

The Pitch

THE CROWD

The Crowd is made up of spectators who ring the boundary while the match is in progress. Not all of them have set out with the intention of watching a game of cricket. Some are having picnics with unruly children. Some have stopped for an absent-minded moment while walking their dogs. Some are wives and girlfriends using the afternoon to top up their suntans and the odd couple lying half in and half out of the bushes or writhing in the long grass have come to lie half in and half out of the bushes or writhe in the long grass.

When fielding try not to become over-interested in these writhing couples or any other spectators' activities that may distract you from the game. If a dog or small child should wander onto the pitch to perform some unsavoury act, ignore it. A chased dog always assumes a game is being played with it and a chased child will only involve its parents.

A crowd may well consist of some unruly elements; these are known as skinheads. Always guard your equipment from these persons during tea interval lest it be removed. Stumps can often disappear. The ordinary skinhead will remove them all, but the creative one will only take two and watch at a distance while you decide how to employ the remaining four.

The Crowd

THE MATCH